HO CHI MINH
Travel Guide

The Ultimate Ho Chi Minh City Guide!
Everything You Need to Know and Must
See Attractions for a Memorable Getaway
in Ho Chi Minh City, Vietnam.

BETTY R. CROSS

COPYRIGHT

The Cafe Apartment

TABLE OF CONTENTS

INTRODUCTION

My Ho Chi Minh City Adventure

I knew I was in for a special adventure as soon as my foot touched the ground of this magnificent city. The vivid history of the city appeared to be told via the busy streets of District 1, where my Ho Chi Minh tour started. The smell of street cuisine wafted down Bui Vien Street, luring me to stop and sample the Banh Mi being sold by a bustling street seller.

With its red-bricked exterior echoing stories of French influence, the Notre Dame Cathedral Basilica of Saigon rose tall in the center of the city. The Central Post Office, which stands next to it and is a monument to the city's blending of the past and contemporary, enthralled me with its colonial-era architecture.

The War Remnants Museum provided a moving tour of Vietnam's past as I proceeded into District 3. Even though the displays were depressing, they served as an important reminder of the Vietnamese people's tenacity and determination.

Leaving the bustle of the city behind, I found the peace of District 10's Le Thi Rieng Park. The tranquil lake, verdant surroundings, and tai chi practitioners portrayed a soothing image that stood in sharp contrast to the bustling activities of District 1.

My nights along Bui Vien were a kaleidoscope of pubs and clubs where the nightlife played out, a symphony of lights and laughter. I couldn't help but get engrossed in the lively atmosphere of the city and its inhabitants.

I was looking for hidden jewels when I came onto the colorful street art that covered the little passages of Pham Ngu Lao's secret alley paintings. Every mural conveyed a tale and enhanced the storyline of the city with a dash of urban art.

Nestled in a peaceful area in District 3, the Jade Emperor Pagoda became my haven. The finely detailed sculptures and the aroma of incense provided a peaceful atmosphere that encouraged introspection.

The city's appeal evolved with the seasons. Springtime Tet festivals brought cheer to the streets, while summertime brought exciting nights on Bui Vien. I discovered rooftop bars by the gentle autumn air, and Saigon River cruises in the winter were a magical experience.

My trip around the city's attractions wasn't the only thing that made up my Ho Chi Minh experience; it was a tapestry made of cultural discoveries, hidden treasures, and kind locals. With every step I took, a new chapter opened up in my experience, turning it into a tale to be treasured and shared with joy.

Welcome to Ho Chi Minh City

Welcome to Ho Chi Minh City, a magical city where history, culture, and modernity all come together to provide an unforgettable travel experience. Locals refer to this dynamic city in southern Vietnam as "Saigon," and it welcomes you to explore its colourful streets, fascinating historical sites, and mouthwatering food.

Overview of Ho Chi Minh City

History Comes Alive: The city of Ho Chi Minh leaves the marks of a turbulent and wealthy past. Relics from the French colonial era, which was once a major centre, may be seen in District 1's architecture. Two surviving reminders of this bygone age are the Central Post Office, an architectural marvel, and the Notre Dame Cathedral Basilica of Saigon, with its recognizable red bricks.

Districts, Diversity, & District 5: The city is a patchwork of diverse districts, each offering a unique flavour. District 3 is a canvas of local life, adorned with vibrant street art and the aroma of street-side Pho stalls. Venture into District 5, Cholon, where the Chinese influence is palpable. This ancient Chinatown unravels a tapestry of temples, markets, and cultural fusion, with the Jade Emperor Pagoda being a Must-Visit.

Culinary Kaleidoscope: Ho Chi Minh City is a culinary paradise. The sounds of street food vendors filling up the streets are audible. Indulge in the cuisine of the area, relishing in

Banh Mi, crisp spring rolls, and fragrant Vietnamese coffee. District 1's Ben Thanh Market is a gourmet haven that provides a mouthwatering sensory experience as well as a chance to interact with the lively street food scene of the city.

River of Lights in District 4: District 4 near the Saigon River becomes a brilliant spectacle when the sun sets. A river cruise provides amazing views of the city skyline, reflecting in the glistening waters an alluring fusion of modernity and history. This encounter captures the spirit of Ho Chi Minh City as it speeds toward the future while embracing its history with elegance.

Planning Your Trip

Ideal Time to Go: While there is always plenty to do in Ho Chi Minh City, visiting during the dry season (December to April) is the best time. The nice weather at this time of the year makes it possible to explore outdoor sites without worrying about rainy days.

How to Get There: The main entry point into the city is Tan Son Nhat International Airport. From all around the globe, it's readily accessible with direct flights and easy connections. Taxis, ride-sharing programs, and airport shuttles all provide convenient transit to the city centre once you arrive.

Accommodation Options: Make thoughtful lodging selections to maximise your experience. Due to its convenient position and close access to important attractions, District 1 is a well-liked option. The city has a variety of alternatives to suit a range of tastes, from five-star hotels to affordable lodgings and distinctive lodgings.

Navigating the City: Scooters dominate the traffic in Ho Chi Minh City, making it seem chaotic as they weave through the streets. Take advantage of the lively environment by exploring on foot or by adopting the native mode of transportation, which includes rickshaws and cyclos. For easy citywide transportation, ride-sharing options and public buses are also easily accessible.

Must-See Attractions & Itineraries: Plan your schedule carefully to get the most out of your trip. Make sure to make stops at well-known locations like the Reunification Palace, the War Remnants Museum, and the busy Bui Vien Street. Organise your visit according to districts, spending time exploring the local customs of District 3, the historical beauty of District 5, and the riverfront appeal of District 4.

Immersion-Based Activities: Take in street cuisine samples, market exploration, and traditional performances to fully immerse oneself in the culture. Through guided tours and museum visits, you may interact with the city's heritage and learn more about Vietnam's past.

To sum up, Ho Chi Minh City is a fabric that is knitted together with strands of history, cultural variety, and contemporary energy. By organising your travel, you may explore the many facets of this vibrant city and guarantee an amazing journey full of surprises and magic.

GETTING THERE

Transportation Options

Ho Chi Minh City is a welcoming city that is easy to travel to, with a variety of transportation alternatives to suit a range of tastes and price points.

Air Travel:
Tan Son Nhat International Airport is the main airport and the starting point of most travels to the city. Ho Chi

Minh City is connected to locations throughout the globe by its busy airport. It is handy for passengers since there are direct flights and well-planned layovers. The airport has all the amenities, currency exchange desks, and transportation services you need to make a seamless transfer into the city once you arrive.

Ground Transportation: Taxis and ride-sharing services provide an easy and convenient way to get to your lodging from the airport. To guarantee a dependable and secure ride, look for respectable taxi services. Another affordable alternative is airport shuttles, particularly if you're staying in a well-known area like District 1.

Local Transport: Because of the distinctive scooters that line the streets, getting about the city is an experience in and of itself. Take a leisurely trip through the busy streets on a cyclo, a classic rickshaw, to embrace the local

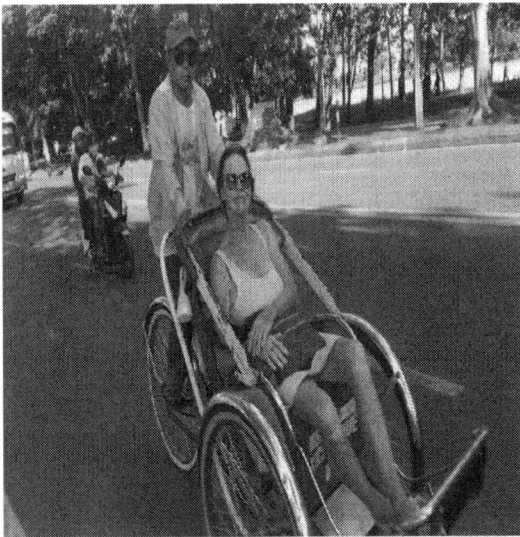

flair. Taxis and ride-sharing services are easily accessible if you want to go at a quicker speed. The city centre is an excellent place to explore on foot since there are a lot of things close by.

Arrival and Departure Tips

Visa Requirements: Make sure you research Vietnam's visa requirements before leaving on your trip. Depending on your country of origin, entrance may need a visa. You may get a visa in advance or at the airport, and the procedure is typically simple. To prevent any surprises, double-check the most recent regulations.

Currency Exchange: You should exchange your money for Vietnamese Dong when you arrive. Obtaining local money is made simple by the presence of ATMs and currency exchange desks at the airport and main neighbourhoods. Since not all establishments take credit cards, it's a good idea to have extra cash on hand for modest purchases.

Local SIM Card: In a new place, staying in touch is essential. For internet access and local calling, think about getting a local SIM card in the city or at the airport. This comes in particularly useful while utilising ride-sharing applications, navigating with maps, and communicating with other passengers.

Accommodation Arrangements: It's crucial to have your accommodation information on hand. Giving the location of your lodging to the driver of a taxi or ride-sharing service guarantees a seamless travel experience. Because language hurdles might sometimes arise while communicating with drivers, it's best to have a written copy or a screenshot on your phone.

Language Tips: Even though many tourist destinations speak English, getting to know a few simple Vietnamese phrases can help you communicate with people and have a better experience. Basic salutations and courteous remarks are always valued and may result in enjoyable exchanges.

Airport Departure Tips: As your journey draws to a close, arrange your exit with simplicity. Due to its popularity, Tan Son Nhat

International Airport is best visited well in advance. Verify the status of your flight, finish any immigration requirements, and set aside time for duty-free shopping or a last-minute bowl of Pho.

Transportation to the Airport: Make prior travel arrangements for the airport, particularly during busy times. Reliable choices include airport shuttles, taxis, and ride-sharing programs. Verify the expected time of arrival to make sure you can easily make it to the airport and prevent any last-minute rush.

In conclusion, using the variety of available transportation alternatives and careful preparation make travelling to and from Ho Chi Minh City a smooth experience. Travel is all part of the experience, and Ho Chi Minh City is ready to reveal its beauty to you, from the thrill of landing to the goodbye upon leaving.

ACCOMMODATION

Your whole trip to Ho Chi Minh City can be influenced by the lodging you choose. Travellers seeking elegance, affordability, or a dash of local character will find enough to choose from in the city.

Hotel Recommendations
District 1: The Heart of Comfort

District 1 is the place to go if you're looking for convenience combined with a hint of elegance. Ensuring proximity to key attractions such as the lively Ben Thanh Market and Notre-Dame Cathedral Basilica of Saigon, this neighbourhood is home to some of the best hotels in the city.

- *Park Hyatt Saigon:* Sophistication emanates from the Park Hyatt Saigon, which is tucked away in the heart of District 1. Sophisticated service, large suites, and a rooftop pool with panoramic views make it the perfect place for anybody looking for an opulent getaway.

- *Caravelle Saigon:* A monument in itself, Caravelle Saigon offers both contemporary conveniences and a historic past. Saigon Saigon, its rooftop bar, offers an unrivalled view of the metropolis. It's a great starting point to explore District 1's offers because of its central position.

- *Rex Hotel Saigon:* Distinguished by its historic appeal, the Rex Hotel is a city landmark. Situated close to the Opera House, it provides a mix of contemporary comfort and traditional grandeur. The rooftop garden is the ideal place to relax after a day of sightseeing.

Budget-Friendly Stays
District 3: Affordable Comfort
District 3 offers a selection of reasonably priced lodging options if your goal is to travel as lightly as possible without sacrificing comfort. While

still being near to the city centre, this zone provides a more genuine and local feel.

- ***Ngoc Linh Hotel:*** This modest hotel offers a tranquil haven in the middle of the city, tucked down a little lane. Budget-conscious guests love it for its clean, comfy accommodations and kind staff.

- ***Alagon Zen Hotel & Spa:*** This charming hotel in District 3 strikes a mix between price and amenities. A friendly environment is created by the attentive service and Zen-inspired decor. Popular sights like the War Remnants Museum are not far away.

- ***Eco Backpackers Hostel:*** This District 3 hostel blends affordability with a lively community vibe, making it ideal for single travellers or those looking for a social setting. It's a terrific idea to make new friends in the rooftop area.

Unique Lodging Experiences
Beyond the Ordinary: Distinctive Stays in Ho Chi Minh City

The Myst Dong Khoi: Located in District 1, The Myst Dong Khoi is a unique place to stay, combining contemporary and French colonial architecture. A mood of mystery and elegance is created by the careful decorating of each space. The rooftop pool offers a calm haven from the busy metropolis.

Container Hostel: If you want to have a very unique experience, think about booking a room in a container hostel.

Hotel JK Container House

In District 4, these converted cargo containers provide a simple and environmentally responsible lodging choice. It's the perfect option for the daring tourist looking for something unique to do.

Villa Song Saigon: Located in District 2, Villa Song Saigon is tucked away along the Saigon River and takes you to a peaceful haven. The boutique hotel offers a tranquil haven from

the bustle of the city thanks to its beautiful gardens, riverfront location, and colonial charm. For those looking for a quiet getaway, it's a hidden treasure.

Take your desired experience into consideration while selecting your lodging. Ho Chi Minh City has something for every taste, whether it is the distinct appeal of unorthodox lodgings, the splendour of District 1, or the affordability of District 3. Not only will your accommodations provide a place to sleep, but they will also play a significant role in your trip, adding to the entire experience of seeing this vibrant city.

EXPLORING DISTRICTS

Ho Chi Minh City is made up of a colourful patchwork of districts, each having its unique character and attractions. Discovering these areas offers a diverse experience, whether you're attracted to the vibrancy of the city centre, the small-town charm of the neighbourhoods, or the historical significance of Chinatown.

District 1: The Heart of the City

Iconic Landmarks: The vibrant District 1 of Ho Chi Minh City is home to several famous

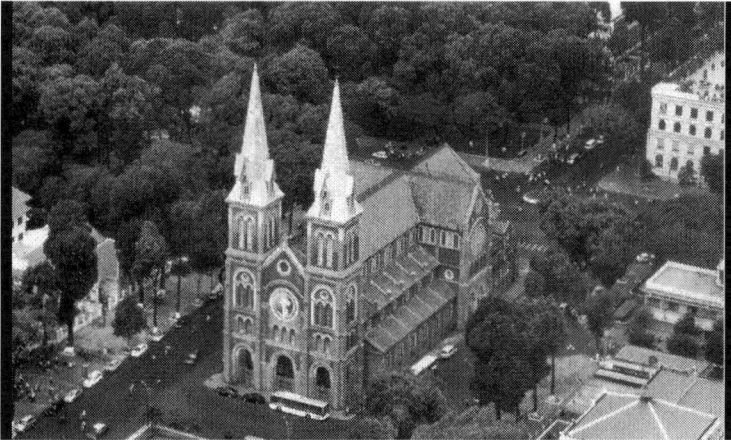

monuments and a vibrant environment. Commence your tour with Saigon's Notre-Dame Cathedral Basilica, a striking red structure that serves as the city's emblem. Gustave Eiffel's Central Post Office, which stands next to it, is a prime example of French colonial architecture.

Bui Vien Street: Experience the lively nightlife on Bui Vien Street as the sun sets. This busy boulevard, which is lined with eateries, bars, and street performers, gives visitors a sense of the vibrancy of the city. It serves as a nexus for both residents and visitors, resulting in a vibrant mingling of cultures.

Ben Thanh Market: You cannot visit District 1 and not see Ben Thanh Market. This vibrant market's sights, sounds, and smells provide a genuine window into local culture. It's a sensory extravaganza and a treasure mine of mementos, with everything from fresh fruit to handcrafted crafts.

Accommodation & Luxury Shopping: There are several different types of lodging in District 1, including boutique hotels and opulent hotels. Dong Khoi Street provides upscale shopping experiences with both local a foreign designer stores if you're an avid shopper.

District 3: Local Culture & Cuisine
Street Art and Local Life: Go to District 3 for a more in-depth look at the culture of the area. This neighbourhood is a colourful canvas of street art that displays the community's inventiveness and resiliency. Explore the little lanes to find undiscovered treasures and see how daily life is carried out.

War Remnants Museum: A must-see in District 3 is the War Remnants Museum, a sobering reminder of Vietnam's past. The exhibitions highlight the Vietnamese people's resiliency and provide a dismal but crucial viewpoint on the Vietnam War.

Image of the War Remnants Museum

Local Cuisine: A cuisine lover's delight is District 3. Taste the real deal Vietnamese food by exploring the neighbourhood restaurants and food carts. From rich Pho to crunchy Banh Mi, every meal narrates a story of tastes that have been handed down through the ages.

Jade Emperor Pagoda: Visit the Jade Emperor Pagoda to fully immerse yourself in District 3's rich cultural diversity. With its elaborate sculptures and carvings, this Taoist temple provides a peaceful haven from the bustle of the city.

District 5: Cholon - Chinatown

Cultural Fusion: Explore the vibrant district of Cholon, District 5, which is the centre of Chinatown. You'll be welcomed by the captivating fusion of Vietnamese and Chinese cultures as soon as you walk in. A distinct atmosphere is created by the architecture's vivid reds and golds as well as the lingering incense aroma.

Binh Tay Market: Discover Cholon's principal market, Binh Tay Market, which is always crowded. The market offers everything from traditional medicines to elaborate handicrafts, and it's a riot of colour and movement. It's a visceral encounter that encapsulates Chinatown.

Thien Hau Temple: Without seeing Thien Hau Temple, a trip to Cholon isn't complete. This evocative temple, which honours the sea goddess, has exquisite Chinese architecture. A mystical and breathtaking experience is created by the minute details and the aroma of burning incense.

District 5's Culinary Delights: Savour the delectable cuisine of Chinatown. The street food vendors and neighbourhood restaurants provide a delicious variety of Chinese-Vietnamese fusion cuisine, ranging from dim sum to flavorful noodle soups. Don't pass up the chance to sample delicacies like Banh Xeo and Hu Tieu.

Other Notable Districts
District 2: Riverside Retreat
Step out of the city and explore District 2. This area, which is well-known for its expat population, has a more relaxed vibe. The cafés and restaurants along the riverbank promenade provide a tranquil haven with a gorgeous view of the Saigon River.

District 4: Riverside Nightlife
Explore District 4 for a fun-filled evening by the sea. With its colourful riverbank pubs and restaurants, the area comes to life at night. Savour a drink along the riverside with the

locals and other tourists as you take in the twinkling city lights.

Phu Nhuan District: Local Markets & Parks

With its vibrant marketplaces and peaceful parks, Phu Nhuan District provides a more authentic experience. A hidden treasure is the Tan Dinh Market, where you may discover unusual items and locally grown products. Le Van Tam Park offers a tranquil haven for early exercise or a leisurely walk.

In Conclusion, in Ho Chi Minh City, every neighbourhood tells a different part of its narrative. The city encourages you to experience its many sides, whether you're drawn to the vibrant energy of District 1, engrossed in the local culture of District 3, transported to a bygone period in Cholon, or finding hidden jewels in less well-known neighbourhoods. Every neighbourhood adds to the complex fabric that makes Ho Chi Minh City a unique travel destination as you explore the streets, savour the cuisine, and take in the history.

CULTURAL EXPERIENCES

Ho Chi Minh City is more than simply a travel destination; it's a living museum that tells the tale of Vietnam through the fusion of art, history, and custom. Explore the cultural mosaic of the city, where each turn reveals a fragment of history and each event speaks to the spirit of the country.

Historical Landmarks

Notre-Dame Cathedral Basilica of Saigon: Saigon's Notre-Dame Cathedral Basilica, towering above District 1, is a remarkable representation of the city. The vivid red bricks, which were brought over from France, illustrate the impact of French colonisation. There's no denying the gravitas of this famous monument when you go closer. Gaze over the Gothic building that carries you back in time, and pause to take in the history.

Reunification Palace: The Reunification Palace, once known as the Independence

Palace, is a living reminder of Vietnam's turbulent past. During the Vietnam War, this stunning building in District 1 functioned as the presidential residence. Discover the moments that moulded the country as you meander around the painstakingly maintained chambers, which include the combat command centre in the basement.

War Remnants Museum: The War Remnants Museum, which is situated in District 3, offers an insightful viewpoint on the Vietnam War. The displays, which include military equipment, images, and first-hand accounts, provide visitors with an intensely moving tour of the nation's history. It's a melancholy but necessary event that promotes empathy and understanding.

Opera House: The Opera House in District 1 will transport you to the splendour of the French colonial period. The magnificent interiors and elaborate architecture capture the grace of a bygone period. Take in the outside or see a show while meandering around the neighbouring area, where the statue of Truong Dinh lends a touch of local flavour.

Museums and Art Galleries

Fine Arts Museum: The Fine Arts Museum located in District 1 offers an immersive experience of Vietnam's cultural legacy. The

museum features a wide range of ornamental arts, sculptures, and paintings from many historical eras. This visual tour, which features both traditional and modern Vietnamese artwork, offers insights into the country's creative development.

Museum of Vietnamese History: Tucked away in District 1, the Museum of Vietnamese History takes you on a tour through the history of the country. Discover antiquities, historical relics, and displays that cover Vietnam's history from the Paleolithic to the Modern Era. The all-encompassing approach of the museum provides a thorough picture of the cultural development of the nation.

Saigon Museum of Contemporary Art: Visit the Saigon Museum of Contemporary Art in District 1 to get a sample of contemporary Vietnamese art. This gallery offers a venue for modern expression by showcasing the works of established and up-and-coming artists. The dynamic of Vietnam's art landscape is reflected in the constantly shifting exhibitions.

Street Art in District 3: District 3's streets serve as a blank canvas for urban expression; it's not simply about museums. Bright street art covers alleyways, walls, and buildings, providing a modern portrayal of the creativity and culture of the area. Enjoy a walk while allowing the street art to tell its tales.

Traditional Performances

Water Puppetry at Golden Dragon Water Puppet Theatre: Visit the Golden Dragon Water Puppet Theater in District 1 to see the captivating art of water puppetry. This centuries-old Vietnamese performance art has puppeteers manipulating puppets on water. Live music complements the vibrant puppets as they narrate stories of history, culture, and everyday life, resulting in an enchanting and family-friendly cultural encounter.

A O Show: Come and see the exciting A O Show, a modern Vietnamese show that combines dance, theatre, and acrobatics. Situated in District 1, this show uses engaging performances to tell the tale of rural Vietnam. It is a unique and strikingly beautiful cultural show due to the blending of traditional and contemporary components.

Traditional Music at The Mist Show: Located in District 7, The Mist Show presents a tasteful fusion of dance, traditional music, and modern technology. The performances, which include stories from many places, highlight

Vietnam's cultural richness. It's an immersive cultural experience because of the compelling environment created by the play of lights and music.

Southern Folk Cake Festival: If you are fortunate enough to be here during the Southern Folk Cake Festival, take part in this lively celebration of classic Vietnamese pastries. Every year, District 8 has a festival that pleasantly combines culture and food. The event provides a wide variety of delicious local foods.

In Conclusion, the cultural offerings of Ho Chi Minh City are a mix of art, history, and performance. Every experience you have broadens your perspective on Vietnam, whether you're learning about the country via historical sites that record its journey, visiting galleries and museums that highlight its creative legacy, or taking in live folklore performances. You'll discover that every area of the city is a blank canvas just ready to tell you its narrative as you explore these cultural treasures.

CULINARY DELIGHTS

Every taste of food in Ho Chi Minh City is a flavour explosion, and the scent of delectable treats wafts from every part of the city. The city provides a sensory-expanding culinary experience, ranging from modest street vendors to fine dining venues.

Street Food Adventures

Banh Mi on Bui Vien Street: Start your exploration of street cuisine with the well-known banh mi. For this Vietnamese sandwich, go to District 1's Bui Vien Street, where booths are often busy. Savoury meats, crunchy veggies, and an assortment of sauces fill freshly baked

baguettes, creating a symphony of sensations. The outcome? the ideal harmony of flavours and textures that characterises Vietnamese street cuisine.

Pho at Pho Hoa Pasteur: A trip through Vietnamese cuisine would not be complete without indulging in a hot bowl of pho. District 1's Pho Hoa Pasteur is well-known for its flavorful soup, fine rice noodles, and soft meat or chicken pieces. To capture the flavour of Vietnamese comfort cuisine, customise your Pho experience by adding fresh herbs, lime, and chile to your bowl.

Bun Thit Nuong in District 3: The street food in District 3 is quite delicious, with the grilled pork noodle salad known as Bun Thit Nuong being one of the best dishes. A variety of fresh herbs, vermicelli

noodles, and the smokey taste of the grilled pork combine to provide a meal that is both filling and invigorating. For a genuine sense of Vietnam's gastronomic variety, try it at neighbourhood vendors.

Saigon Coffee: Don't miss the opportunity to experience Saigon's renowned coffee culture. Grab a cup of classic Vietnamese coffee by strolling into a nearby coffee shop or by sitting down at a café on the street. Fueling the city's fast pace, the robust, thick coffee is served with sweetened condensed milk and makes for a delicious caffeine dose.

Top Restaurants

Nha Hang Ngon: Culinary Wonderland

Foodies will adore Nha Hang Ngon in District 1, which offers a wide variety of gastronomic experiences. Located in a villa dating back to the colonial period, this restaurant offers a wide selection of Vietnamese cuisine under one roof. Every meal, from delicate spring rolls to delicious pho, is made with flair and authenticity, providing a feast for the senses.

Quan An Ngon: Street Food in Style

In District 1, Quan An Ngon turns street food into a sophisticated dining experience. This restaurant, which is situated in a lovely courtyard, has a large menu that highlights popular Vietnamese street food

©AsiaWebDirect

dishes. For those looking for a pleasant environment with a taste of local delicacies, this place is a must-visit because of its dynamic atmosphere and great food.

The Deck Saigon: Riverside Elegance

The Deck Saigon, situated in District 2 along the Saigon River, is a great place to escape the bustle of the city and eat in elegance. This elegant restaurant has a panoramic outlook and a calm atmosphere. The cuisine creates a refined and memorable dining experience by combining traditional Vietnamese ingredients with tastes from across the world.

Unique Food Experiences
Floating Markets in the Mekong Delta: Visit the floating markets in the Mekong Delta, which are just a short drive from Ho Chi Minh City, and go on a unique gastronomic

excursion. Take a boat ride through lively market places where nearby merchants provide fresh food and regional delicacies. Indulge in the vibrant ambiance of these floating marketplaces while sampling exotic fruits, coconut sweets, and savoury delicacies.

Cooking Classes in Ho Chi Minh City:
Consider enrolling in a cooking class in Ho Chi Minh City if you want some practical practice. Local chefs will teach you the technique of creating Vietnamese food and will walk you through its subtleties. These programs provide a better knowledge of the products and methods that go into making Vietnamese cuisine great and range from market trips to cooking sessions.

Hidden Alleyway Restaurants: Explore the less-travelled alleys in Districts 4 or 5 to find hidden treasures, which are neighbourhood eateries nestled away from the busy main streets. These little restaurants often provide some of the most delicious and genuine food. Talk to people, use your senses, and you'll discover hidden culinary gems that capture the essence of Ho Chi Minh City.

In conclusion, the food scene in Ho Chi Minh City is an explosion of tastes, textures, and customs. Every meal becomes an exploration of Vietnam's diverse culinary legacy, whether you're going on a street food trip, eating at fine dining establishments, or trying out novel culinary experiences. Taste the city's varied and delectable choices, from the sizzle of street-side barbecues to the sophistication of riverfront restaurants, making every culinary moment an exceptional experience.

SHOPPING IN HO CHI MINH CITY

Ho Chi Minh City is a shopping haven, with vibrant marketplaces, chic boutiques, and one-of-a-kind handicraft stores enticing with a wide variety of finds. Regardless of your inclination for unique or locally sourced mementos, the city has a wide range of shopping options to suit every taste.

Local Markets

Ben Thanh Market: A trip to Ben Thanh Market is a must for every shopping excursion in Ho Chi Minh City. This famous market, which is in District 1, is a hive of activity. Wander through the aisles brimming with vendors offering everything from fresh fruit and regional specialties to apparel and accessories. Strike a deal with amiable sellers and take in the vibrant vibe of this busy marketplace.

Binh Tay Market in Cholon: Go to Binh Tay Market in Cholon, District 5, for a more authentic and local shopping experience. With an emphasis on wholesale products, this market is a veritable gold mine of merchandise. Stroll around little alleys crowded with vendors selling fabrics, spices, and elaborate handicrafts. The genuineness of the market offers an insight into the manner of living in the area.

Saigon Square: District 1's Saigon Square is a well-liked spot for bargain shoppers. There is a large selection of goods available at this indoor market, such as electronics, clothes, and accessories. The bustling environment and inexpensive pricing heighten the joy of discovering amazing offers. It's a great place to get stylish clothing at reasonable costs.

Boutique Shops

Dong Khoi Street: Boutique stores selling premium goods and designer labels along District 1's Dong Khoi Street, catering to customers looking for a more upmarket shopping experience. This chic strip, which offers both local and foreign designers, is a refuge for affluent shoppers. Take a peek at chic stores, indulge in a little window shopping, or treat yourself to something elegantly classy.

L'Usine: Situated in District 1, L'Usine is a stylish concept that blends a restaurant, café, and carefully chosen store into one cohesive space. The store sells carefully chosen apparel, accoutrements, and household goods. For those looking for unusual and fashionable findings, this place is a unique destination because of the meticulously selected objects that showcase a fusion of Vietnamese workmanship and modern style.

Souvenirs and Handicrafts
Hem 15A: District 1's Artisan Collective
To get genuine Vietnamese handicrafts and souvenirs, go to District 1's Hem 15A. An artisan association that showcases the creations of regional craftspeople is this undiscovered treasure. Every item, from distinctive home décor pieces to handcrafted jewellery and textiles, reflects the artistry of Vietnamese handicraft. It's the perfect location to locate sentimental mementos that encapsulate the spirit of the local way of life.

XQ Hand Embroidery: Intricate Vietnamese Artistry

XQ Hand Embroidery is a must-visit if you value fine workmanship. This District 1 store specialises in hand-embroidered artwork made by talented Vietnamese designers. These exquisite and heartfelt keepsakes are made from intricately embroidered motifs depicting Vietnamese culture and scenery.

The Propaganda Bistro: Artistic Souvenirs with a Twist

In addition to providing a great eating experience, the Propaganda Bistro in District 1 allows purchasing distinctive mementos. The store sells oddball goods with a contemporary take on traditional Vietnamese design characteristics. These creative mementos, which range from t-shirts to accessories, are fun ways to reminisce about your trip to Ho Chi Minh City.

In conclusion, Ho Chi Minh City offers a shopping experience that fulfils the needs of all customers. Discovering distinctive handicrafts in obscure stores, sulking in upscale fashion on

Dong Khoi Street, or exploring the colourful chaos of local markets—the city beckons you to unearth gems that showcase its artistic and cultural diversity. So go shopping, grin while haggling, and take home a little bit of the lively energy of Ho Chi Minh City.

OUTDOOR ACTIVITIES

Many fun outdoor activities in Ho Chi Minh City allow you to experience both the natural beauty and the bustle of the city. The outdoor activities available here are just as varied as the city itself, ranging from serene parks and picturesque river cruises to exciting day adventures.

Parks and Gardens

Le Van Tam Park: Nestled in the centre of District 1, Le Van Tam Park offers a peaceful haven from the bustle of the city. This urban paradise offers a calm area ideal for an early morning workout or a leisurely walk. It is a well-liked location for both residents and tourists looking for a quiet getaway in the middle of the busy city because of its lush vegetation, covered walkways, and open areas.

Tao Dan Park: District 1's Tao Dan Park is a cultural and recreational oasis that captures the dynamic essence of Ho Chi Minh City. In addition to being a peaceful haven, the park serves as a meeting spot for neighbourhood residents interested in a range of pursuits, such as bird watching and conventional fitness. Take in the vibrant ambiance as you stroll about the garden areas, particularly in the early morning or late afternoon.

District 7 Promenade: Visit the District 7 Promenade if you want to see beautiful waterfront scenery. This serene haven from the busy city centre is located along the Saigon River in a lovely region. Enjoy the beauty of the river and the city skyline by going for a stroll or a leisurely bike ride along the riverfront. Cafes along the promenade make it the ideal place to unwind and enjoy the moment.

River Cruises

Saigon River Cruise: Take a ride along the Saigon River for a fascinating nighttime experience. As the city lights come up and the river takes on a lovely glow, take a leisurely cruise down it. Many companies provide supper cruises where you may taste authentic Vietnamese food and take in the breathtaking scenery and live music. This romantic tour offers a distinctive viewpoint of the skyline of Ho Chi Minh City.

Mekong Delta Day Cruise: Take a day trip around the Mekong Delta to spend some time away from the city. Discover the Mekong Delta's numerous canals, verdant surroundings, and quaint communities. These excursions often feature stops at regional markets, boat rides along winding canals, and chances to see how riverbank towns go about their everyday lives. Only a short drive from Ho Chi Minh City, it offers the ideal fusion of nature and culture.

Cu Chi Tunnels Boat & Bike Tour: Take a boat and bike journey to the Cu Chi Tunnels to combine adventure and history. Travel down the Saigon River to the Cu Chi region, where you may tour the well-known tunnels that were utilised in the Vietnam War. After the historical tour, ride a bike into the picturesque countryside, passing through quaint towns and verdant vistas. This trip provides a unique fusion of historical knowledge with outdoor experience.

Day Trips and Excursions

Vung Tau Beach Day Trip: Take a day trip to Vung Tau, a seaside city a short distance from Ho Chi Minh City, for a beach getaway. Once you arrive, you may relax on sandy beaches, tour the Christ the King monument for expansive views, and savour fresh seafood at coastal eateries. The trip takes you through magnificent landscapes. For those who are looking for sun, beach, and sea, Vung Tau provides a tranquil getaway.

Can Gio Mangrove Forest: The Can Gio Mangrove Forest, a UNESCO Biosphere Reserve, is a paradise for nature lovers. This natural area, which is about an hour outside the city, is home to a wide variety of plants and animals. Explore the Can Gio Monkey Island, see animals, and take a boat ride through the mangrove waterways. For those who like the outdoors, the unique ecology and abundant vegetation make for a rejuvenating day trip.

Cao Dai Temple and Cu Chi Tunnels Tour: Set off on a day tour that blends historical lessons with cultural experience. See the Cao Dai Temple, an intriguing temple renowned for its colourful rituals and distinctive architectural design. After that, explore Vietnam's combat past by visiting the Cu Chi Tunnels. With the entire experience offered by this trip, you may fully immerse yourself in historical importance as well as cultural richness.

In conclusion, the outdoors in Ho Chi Minh metropolis beckons you to discover the bustling cityscape, tranquil parks, and breathtaking natural vistas that envelop the metropolis. Every outdoor experience gives a different viewpoint of Vietnam's dynamic culture and scenery, whether you're sailing down the Saigon River, meandering through verdant parks, or taking day excursions to neighbouring locations. So slip on some comfy shoes, enjoy the fresh air, and watch as Ho Chi Minh City's many outdoor activities reveal themselves to you.

NIGHTLIFE & ENTERTAINMENT

Ho Chi Minh City becomes a buzzing playground for people looking for dynamic nightlife and interesting entertainment as the sun sets over the busy streets. The city offers much for any nighttime adventurer, from hip pubs and clubs to cultural performances that highlight the rich legacy and bustling evening markets.

Bars and Nightclubs

Bui Vien Street: Visit District 1's Bui Vien Street to get a taste of Ho Chi Minh City's nightlife. The core of bars, pubs, and nightclubs is this lively district. Bui Vien offers everything you could want, including dance floors, rooftop views, and live music. Stroll down the bustling street, visit different establishments, and interact with the residents and other tourists who are enjoying the vibrant environment.

Chill Skybar: Head to District 1's Chill Skybar for a classy nightlife experience with panoramic views. This bar is located on the rooftop of a skyscraper and has an opulent atmosphere. Savour inventive drinks, soak in the stunning view, and groove to the soothing music. For those looking for a more sophisticated and fashionable evening, the trendy atmosphere makes it the perfect place.

Saigon Rooftop Bars: Several rooftop pubs in Ho Chi Minh City provide stunning views of the city's cityscape. Look at places like the Rooftop Bar Saigon Saigon, which is housed in the recognizable Caravelle Saigon. The city lights glitter below, creating a stunning scene at these hilltop sites. Rooftop bars provide an unforgettable way to see the city after dark, whether you're drinking drinks or spending a calm evening with friends.

Cultural Shows

Golden Dragon Water Puppet Theater: Visit the Golden Dragon Water Puppet Theater in District 1 to explore the fascinating art of water puppetry. This centuries-old traditional

Vietnamese art form has puppeteers manipulating puppets on water. Live music complements the vibrant puppets as they narrate stories about history, mythology, and everyday life. The captivating and family-friendly entertainment experience is produced by the marriage of cultural storytelling with expert puppetry.

A O Show: Come and see the exciting A O Show, a modern Vietnamese show that combines dance, theatre, and acrobatics. Situated in District 1, this show uses engaging performances to tell the tale of rural Vietnam. It is a unique and visually spectacular cultural event that offers an interesting evening of entertainment because of the mix of traditional and contemporary components.

The Mist Show: See The Mist Show, a mesmerising production that blends traditional music, dance, and cutting-edge technology, by travelling to District 7. The performance, which takes place in a contemporary theatre, combines stories from many parts of Vietnam. It is an immersive cultural experience that stimulates the senses thanks to the compelling environment created by the play of lights and music.

Evening Markets

Ben Thanh Night Market: Visit District 1's Ben Thanh Night Market to continue your shopping spree into the evening. This lively market comes to life as the day gives way to night with colourful kiosks offering a wide range of items. For those who like to shop under the stars, the market provides a vibrant environment with everything from apparel and accessories to souvenirs and regional foods. Strike a deal with sellers and take in the vibrant atmosphere of this well-known night market.

District 4 Night Market: Discover the District 4 Night Market, a gathering place for the locals to enjoy delicious street cuisine and shopping in the evenings. With vendors offering regional delicacies, apparel, and fresh vegetables, this market provides a more genuine experience. It's a great chance to meet people, eat street food, and learn about the vivid tastes of Vietnamese food in a colorful environment.

Saigon Flea Market: Visit the Saigon Flea Market for a more unique and independent experience. This market, which rotates venues, has a variety of antique goods, handcrafted goods, and unusual treasures. Take in the laid-back vibe and live music as you peruse kiosks showcasing unique gifts from local designers and craftsmen.

In conclusion, the entertainment and nightlife of Ho Chi Minh City provide a diverse range of choices to suit every taste. The city comes alive after dark, whether you're wandering through bright evening markets, taking in cultural concerts, or discovering the lively pubs of Bui Vien Street. To have amazing experiences in the centre of Vietnam's nightlife, take advantage of the many entertainment options available as the night draws in and let the spirit of the city lead you.

PRACTICAL TIPS

A lovely trip, exploring Ho Chi Minh City may be made much more fun by keeping in mind some useful advice about local customs, safety, and money.

Currency and Money Matters

Vietnamese Dong (VND): The Vietnamese Dong (VND) is the official currency of Ho Chi Minh City. For local transactions, it is preferable to have Dong on hand, even if some establishments could take US dollars or credit cards. It's advisable to carry a combination of small and big denominations for different types of needs, and currency exchange facilities are easily accessible.

ATMs and Cash Withdrawals: With so many of them scattered around the city, ATMs provide a practical means of taking out cash in Dong. ATMs accept the majority of major credit and debit cards; nevertheless, to prevent any problems with card transactions, you must notify your bank of your travel schedule. Look for ATMs connected to large banks to ensure dependable service.

Bargaining: It's customary to haggle at marketplaces and smaller stores. It's customary in the area, and vendors often anticipate some haggling. Remember to find a medium ground and approach it with a polite demeanour. However, pricing is often set at bigger venues, such as restaurants.

Safety Precautions

Traffic Awareness: Ho Chi Minh City is well-known for its frantic street traffic, which is made up of cyclos, vehicles, and scooters. When crossing roads, use care and observe the traffic pattern; moving at a steady speed without making abrupt moves is usually beneficial. Crossing the street with traffic becomes a rhythmic dance if you look both ways and keep eye contact with them.

Pickpocket Awareness: Even though Ho Chi Minh City is a secure city overall, it's advisable to watch out for pickpockets in busy places like marketplaces. Use anti-theft bags, keep your possessions safe, and refrain from putting expensive stuff on show. Keep an eye out for yourself, particularly in popular tourist areas, and keep critical papers in hotel safes.

Hygiene Precautions: Ho Chi Minh City's tropical environment may be warm and muggy, so it's important to drink enough water. Avoid ice in street food unless it comes from a reputable source, drink bottled or filtered water, and maintain good hygiene. Bring tissues and hand sanitizer in case the facilities don't always have them on hand.

Local Etiquette

Respect for Customs: Your visit to Ho Chi Minh City would be more enjoyable if you adopted the local ways. Wear modest clothing, covering your knees and shoulders, when you visit pagodas or temples. When you enter a person's house or certain places of business, take off your shoes. Locals value maintaining a courteous manner, particularly at places of worship.

Greetings: Courtesies are highly valued in Vietnamese culture. Saying "xin chào" (pronounced sin chow) is a polite greeting. It is courteous to address someone with titles like "Mr." or "Mrs." and then the family name. An acknowledging nod or small bend of the head is customary.

Dining Etiquette: In Ho Chi Minh City, sharing meals with family is the norm while eating. Don't be scared to experiment with different tastes and always use serving utensils instead of personal ones. It's customary to hold off on eating until the host or the oldest child has finished. You feel satiated when there is not much food left on your plate.

In Conclusion, Ho Chi Minh City is a city of contrasts, where vibrant modernity coexists with age-old customs. You can traverse the streets, interact with the locals, and make your vacation memorable and courteous by keeping these helpful pointers in mind. These helpful hints can improve your trip through the centre of Vietnam, whether it's knowing the local money, being alert in busy marketplaces, or accepting traditional practices.

SAMPLE ITINERARIES

With its energetic streets and priceless cultural artefacts, Ho Chi Minh City has plenty to offer every kind of visitor. These itineraries will help you see everything that the city has to offer, whether you have a day, a weekend, or a longer visit.

One Day in Ho Chi Minh City

- *Morning:* Start the day in District 1's Notre-Dame Cathedral Basilica of Saigon. Admire the recognizable red-bricked façade and learn about the building's fascinating past. Visit the Central Post Office, a stunning edifice from the colonial period next to the cathedral, where you may mail postcards or just take in the beauty.

- *Late Morning:* Explore the War Remnants Museum in District 3. Discover more about Vietnam's past with the help of compelling displays and preserved military equipment. The museum offers a grim but necessary viewpoint on the Vietnam War and its effects on the nation.

- **Lunch:** To experience the delicacies of the region, visit Bui Vien Street in District 1. Savour the deliciousness of Banh Mi, a Vietnamese sandwich. There are many selections available from street-side booths, so you may enjoy the delectable simplicity of Vietnamese street cuisine.

- **Afternoon:** Take a leisurely walk along the Saigon River in District 2. Relax and take in the beautiful scenery at one of the riverbank cafés. In contrast to the busy city centre, District 2 has a more serene vibe. Enjoy a coffee or a cool beverage by the lake as you take in the tranquillity.

- **Late Afternoon:** Visit the Cu Chi Tunnels to immerse yourself in history. Investigate the Viet Cong's underground network from the Vietnam War. Learn about the tenacity and ingenuity of the Vietnamese people. A thorough appreciation of the tunnels' importance may be gained via guided tours, which are situated around one hour from the city centre.

- *Evening:* Head back to District 1 to enjoy a lively evening on Bui Vien Street. Discover the unique blend of taverns, pubs, and clubs. Bui Vien provides a wide variety of alternatives, regardless of your preference for a vibrant dance floor or live music. Take in the vibrant environment and socialise with both locals and other tourists.

Weekend Getaway
Day 1: District 1 Exploration
- *Morning:* Take a tour of the energetic District 1 to kick off your weekend. Begin in the Ben Thanh Market, where you may browse for local items and souvenirs. Indulge in a substantial breakfast at one of the local food carts.

- *Late Morning:* Take in Vietnam's cultural legacy by visiting the Fine Arts Museum in District 1. The museum features a wide range of ornamental arts, sculptures, and paintings from many historical eras.

- *Lunch:* For a varied gastronomic experience, head to Nha Hang Ngon. This quaint restaurant in District 1 serves a range of Vietnamese meals.

- *Afternoon:* Visit the Reunification Palace in the afternoon to learn about Ho Chi Minh City's past. Investigate the conserved chambers, including the subterranean battle command centre. For a peaceful day, take a stroll around Tao Dan Park, which is nearby.

- *Evening:* Enjoy a riverfront dining experience at District 2's The Deck Saigon. Savour a fusion of foreign tastes with traditional Vietnamese ingredients.

Day 2: Cu Chi Tunnels & Cultural Shows

- *Morning:* Head to the Cu Chi Tunnels for a half-day excursion. Discover the historical importance of the tunnels and the inventiveness of the Vietnamese people throughout the conflict as you explore them.

- *Lunch:* Savour regional cuisines with a local meal close to the Cu Chi Tunnels.

- *Afternoon:* Head back to District 1 and spend a leisurely day at a nearby spa.

- *Evening:* Take in a cultural performance at District 1's A O Show or the Golden Dragon Water Puppet Theatre. These shows provide a fascinating fusion of modern and traditional art.

Extended Stay Options
Week 1: District Exploration

- ***Days 1-3:*** Spend the first three days thoroughly investigating District 1. Visit local markets, museums, and historic buildings. Explore this busy district's hidden charms and sample a variety of street delicacies.

- ***Days 4-5:*** Continue your tour by visiting District 3, which is renowned for its regional food and culture. Explore the colourful alleyways, eat traditional Vietnamese food, and see the Jade Emperor Pagoda.

Week 2: Extended Excursions

- ***Days 6-7:*** Spend a day at the beach by travelling to Vung Tau. Savour excellent seafood, tour the Christ the King monument, and unwind on beautiful beaches.

- ***Days 8–10:*** Take a three-day tour into the Mekong Delta. Discover floating markets, go through tiny canals, and take in the delta's distinct way of life.

Week 3: Relaxation & Reflection
- *Days 11–14:* Relax in District 7 for the last few days of your prolonged visit. Savour the elegant restaurants, contemporary facilities, and picturesque waterfront views. Take a moment to review your trip to Ho Chi Minh City and feel the vibrant spirit of the city one final time.

In conclusion, Ho Chi Minh City reveals its treasures at your speed, whether you are here for a day, a weekend, or a longer period. From historical insights and cultural discoveries to exciting nightlife and picturesque excursions, these itineraries provide a wide variety of experiences for all types of travellers. Thus, bring your curiosity, enjoy the uniqueness of the area, and allow Ho Chi Minh City to enchant you on your travels.

HIDDEN GEMS

The adventurous tourist will find a wealth of hidden gems in Ho Chi Minh City. There are hidden gems and insider advice from residents that may be found outside the well-travelled routes, adding a more genuine touch to your exploration of this vibrant city.

Off-the-Beaten-Path Attractions

Le Thi Rieng Park: Nestled in District 10, Le Thi Rieng Park is a tranquil haven away from the bustle of the city. This undiscovered treasure provides a serene haven with lush vegetation, lovely walking trails, and a lake. Locals use it as a preferred location for tai chi classes, relaxing picnics, and early workouts. Enjoy some time away from the busy streets and lose yourself in this little-known park's peace.

The Café Apartment: For those who like both coffee and art, the Café Apartment is a special hidden treasure located in the centre of

District 1. Nestled inside a structure from the colonial period, this area has a floor-by-floor arrangement of unique, modest coffee shops. Discover secret alcoves with artwork, antique furniture, and a laid-back bohemian vibe by exploring the winding stairs. It's a fun diversion from the busy streets below.

Pham Ngu Lao Hidden Alley Murals: Explore the obscure lanes of Pham Ngu Lao in District 1 to discover a colourful world of street art. These little alleyways become outdoor galleries with the addition of murals and graffiti. Every piece of art conveys a narrative and embodies the imagination and energy of regional artists. Enjoy a leisurely journey along these secret passageways, where fresh examples of urban art may be found around every corner.

The Observatory: Go to District 4's The Observatory for expansive vistas that are unobstructed by the congested roofs. Locals love this hidden treasure, a rooftop pub with a

1

laid-back vibe that is popular among them. Take in the breathtaking view of the Saigon River and the city skyline while sipping a cocktail. For those looking for a more sedate atmosphere, The Observatory provides a more laid-back and genuine rooftop experience.

Jade Emperor Pagoda: Get away from the throng and explore District 3's Jade Emperor Pagoda. Nestled in a serene community, this

undiscovered treasure is a Taoist temple filled with exquisite sculptures and carvings. A calm environment is created by the incense smell and the quiet ambiance. Take in the spiritual ambiance of this lesser-known cultural treasure while marvelling at the holy relics.

Insider Tips from Locals

Alleyway Eateries: Locals often choose little cafes tucked away in alleyways to places packed with tourists when it comes to real Vietnamese food. Go through the small streets of District 4 or District 5 to find some hidden treasures in the food scene. Delicious, locally-owned restaurants provide a chance to enjoy authentic, home-cooked Vietnamese food away from the major thoroughfares.

Motorbike Exploration: If you want to feel like a local, you might think about hiring a motorcycle. The streets of Ho Chi Minh City may seem hectic at first, but riding a motorcycle around the city lets you discover unusual districts and secret spots. Go with the flow of traffic, explore lesser-known neighbourhoods, and find the true appeal of the city outside of the well-known tourist attractions.

Early Morning Markets: Get up early and visit the neighbourhood markets to get a sense of Ho Chi Minh City's real everyday existence. Early mornings bring a vivid tapestry of fresh food, local merchants, and the steady bustle of morning activity to markets like Cho Ben Thanh and Cho Binh Tay. Before the day is out, interact with people, eat some street cuisine, and feel the pulse of the city.

Hidden Book Cafés: There are several little hidden book cafés in Ho Chi Minh City that provide a literary haven from the bustle of the city. Book enthusiasts will find the ideal haven at establishments like District 3's Dream Beans Coffee and The Hidden Elephant Bookstore, which combine a warm atmosphere with bookshelves. Enjoy a cup of coffee, get lost in a good book, and discover the more sedate side of the city.

Saigon's Secret Bars: Locals are aware that some of the city's greatest bars may be found behind modest facades. Visit locations like The Alley Cocktail Bar in District 3 or Secret Garden in District 1 to learn more about the speakeasy culture. These undiscovered jewels provide a more private and distinctive drinking experience; they often have inventive drinks and chic decor but are still unknown to the general public.

In conclusion, Remember to take detours and explore the hidden jewels that provide a taste of true local experiences as you make your way through Ho Chi Minh City's busy streets. These hidden jewels guarantee that your trip to Ho Chi Minh City is both enlightening and distinctively yours, whether you want to explore urban oases, find street art, or heed expert recommendations for gastronomic excursions. Thus, explore the less travelled areas, engage with the populace, and let the city's best-kept secrets reveal themselves to you.

HO CHI MINH CITY IN EVERY SEASON

Due to its tropical climate, Ho Chi Minh City has a pleasant and inviting environment all year round. There is something delicious waiting for you in this energetic city throughout the year, as each season offers its charm and distinctive experiences.

Spring

Welcoming the Lunar New Year (Tet): In Ho Chi Minh City, Tet, or the Lunar New Year, is celebrated in the spring. With colourful decorations, customary performances, and a bustling atmosphere, the city comes to life. Take a stroll around District 5, which is home to Cholon, the city's Chinatown, and see the busy bustle as residents get ready for the celebrations. Take part in the festivities, enjoy unique Tet cuisine, and feel the exuberance of fresh beginnings.

Mild Weather & Blooming Gardens: The warm temperatures of spring, which span from February to April, make it the perfect season for exploring. Visit District 1's Le Van Tam Park for a vibrant background created by blossoming flowers. Take a stroll, see people doing tai chi, and welcome the season's revitalising vitality. Springtime is ideal for outdoor pursuits, such as exploring hidden treasures in the city or going on cultural outings.

Summer

Tropical Heat and Festive Vibes: June through August is Ho Chi Minh City's summer, with mild weather and sporadic downpours. Savour the tropical heat while discovering the lively vitality of the city. District 1's Bui Vien Street comes alive in the evenings with street entertainers, outdoor cafés, and a celebratory vibe. Indulge in local cuisine, sip on a cool beverage, and take in the vibrant summer vibe of the city.

Mekong Delta Adventures: Take a day excursion to the Mekong Delta to avoid the heat of the city. Explore verdant fruit orchards, go to floating marketplaces, and take a cruise along the labyrinthine canals. Tropical fruits are in season throughout the summer, and visiting the Mekong Delta is a lovely way to experience the freshest food available. An ideal summertime outing, the refreshing river wind offers a nice counterpoint to the heated metropolis.

Autumn

Mild Temperatures and Festivals: Ho Chi Minh City has temperate temperatures and a lovely wind throughout the autumn season, which runs from September to November. It's the perfect time of year for outdoor recreation and cultural adventure. See the Jade Emperor Pagoda in District 3, where the elegant architecture and peaceful atmosphere provide a peaceful haven. Fall is also the time of year for several cultural events, which provide an opportunity to see customs and performances.

District 1 Rooftop Views: When the weather warms up, go to District 1's rooftop bars for breathtaking views of the metropolis. Situated atop the Caravelle Saigon, the Saigon Saigon Rooftop Bar provides expansive views of the city below. Savour a drink in the cool evening air while taking in the splendour of Ho Chi Minh City's changing leaves and the city lights.

Winter

Mild Winters and Cultural Experiences: Ho Chi Minh City has moderate winter temperatures and sporadic chilly nights from December to February. It's a fantastic time to visit historical sites and engage in cultural activities. For more information on Vietnam's past, stop by the War Remnants Museum in District 3. It's more pleasant to explore outdoor sights and have in-depth conversations about the city's heritage in the colder weather.

Saigon River Cruises: Embark on a Saigon River cruise to discover the captivating allure of wintry nights. Enjoying the city lights and the lit skyline while cruising down the river is more enjoyable with the lower temperatures. Dinner cruises are a popular option that gives a peaceful and romantic way to round off your day in Ho Chi Minh City.

In conclusion, Ho Chi Minh City is a year-round destination that offers a wide variety of activities in every season. The city changes its beauty according to the season, whether you're enjoying the rich cultural offerings of autumn, the tropical heat of summer, the joyful emotions of Tet in the spring, or the warm winters with nightly river cruises. Thus, regardless of the season, be sure to pack appropriately, accept the local way of life, and let Ho Chi Minh City reveal its charm.

CONCLUSION

As our tour of Ho Chi Minh City's busy streets and hidden gems comes to an end, it's clear that this vibrant city is a patchwork of contrasts, customs, and contemporary energy. Ho Chi Minh City welcomes you to experience all of its facets, from the historical sites that tell the story of the city's rich history to the undiscovered treasures.

Each encounter adds a brushstroke to the vibrant painting of this Vietnamese jewel, whether you've stared at the Notre Dame Cathedral Basilica of Saigon, explored the history at the War Remnants Museum, or enjoyed the delicacies of street cuisine on Bui Vien Street.

The areas of the city, each with its distinct personality, provide a wide variety of activities. Ho Chi Minh City reveals its riches for all kinds of travellers, from the vibrant energy of District

1 to the cultural diversity of District 3 to the serene havens of District 7.

Eateries tucked away in alleyways, fine dining establishments, and street food excursions all promise culinary thrills. The city's varied culinary scene makes a mark, whether you've had Banh Mi on the streets or dinner with a view of the Saigon River.

Vietnamese culture is reflected in a variety of cultural activities, from modern AO performances to traditional water puppet plays. The parks and open areas across the city provide a calm diversion from the bustle of the city and opportunities for introspection and leisure.

Ho Chi Minh City's charm is ever-evolving, making each visit an unforgettable experience. The city's enthusiasm is contagious all year long, whether you've celebrated Tet in the bright spring, welcomed the tropical heat of summer, relished the gentle autumn air, or encountered the chilly nights of winter.

You've had a peek of the city beyond the guidebooks via the shared hidden jewels and insider knowledge, exploring off-the-beaten-path sites and accepting local knowledge. These gems give your trip a unique touch and help you make memories that go beyond the standard tourist encounter.

Ho Chi Minh City is an entire experience, not just a place to visit, thanks to its kind people, vibrant culture, and welcoming vibe. Take with you the memories of its colourful streets, its delectable food, and the kindness of its people as you wish this enthralling city goodnight. Remember that Ho Chi Minh City will always be waiting to welcome you back with open arms, regardless of whether you depart with a work of traditional art, a tale from a secret alleyway, or just a heart full of memories. Until then, may your travels bring you joy, and may the spirit of this amazing city accompany you on all of your trips. Safe journeys, and see you again in the heart of Vietnam.

APPENDIX

Essential Vietnamese Phrases
- Hello: Xin chào (Sin chow)
- Thank you: Cảm ơn (Gahm uhn)
- Yes: Vâng (Vahng)
- No: Không (Khohng)
- Excuse me/ I'm sorry: Xin lỗi (Sin loy)
- Goodbye: Tạm biệt (Tam byet)
- Please: Làm ơn (Lam uhn)
- How much is this?: Bao nhiêu tiền? (Bow nyew tyen?)
- Where is...?: Ở đâu là...? (Uh dow la...?)
- I don't understand: Tôi không hiểu (Toy khohng hyew)

Useful Contacts
- Emergency Services: 113
- Police: 113
- Fire Department: 114
- Ambulance: 115
- Tourist Information Hotline: 102
- Lost and Found at Tan Son Nhat International Airport: +84 28 3848 5383

Resources

Tourist Information Centers: For directions, pamphlets, and help, stop by the Tourist Information Centers in District 1.

Currency Exchange: Major banks and approved exchange offices provide trustworthy currency exchange services.

Transportation: For easy and secure transportation, make use of reliable ride-sharing applications like Grab. Taxis and local buses are also easily accessible.

Health & Safety: Families looking for medical help can think about Family Medical Practice (District 1) or FV Hospital (District 7).

Embassies: Get in touch with your embassy in case of an emergency or misplaced papers. District 1 is home to the U.S. Consulate General, and the city is home to many other embassies.

Wi-Fi Hotspots: Numerous cafés, eateries, and public areas provide free Wi-Fi so you can stay connected.

Weather Updates: For the most recent predictions, particularly during the rainy season, which runs from May to October, check your local weather updates.

Local Etiquette: Say "Xin chào" (greeting with a smile) and observe traditions by taking off your shoes while entering houses and places of worship.

Keep in mind that Ho Chi Minh City is a friendly place to visit, and using these tools and expressions will make your trip more pleasurable and seamless while you explore this energetic city. These necessities will make excellent travelling companions, whether you're seeing historical sites, sampling regional cuisine, or need help. Travel safely!

Printed in Great Britain
by Amazon